Peer Pressure

Loveland, Colorado

Group's R.E.A.L. Guarantee to you:

This Group resource incorporates our R.E.A.L. approach to ministry—one that encourages long-term retention and life transformation. It's ministry that's:

Relational
Because learner-to-learner interaction enhances learning and builds Christian friendships.

Experiential
Because what learners experience through discussion and action sticks with them up to 9 times longer than what they simply hear or read.

Applicable
Because the aim of Christian education is to equip learners to be both hearers and doers of God's Word.

Learner-based
Because learners understand and retain more when the learning process takes into consideration how they learn best.

Peer Pressure

Visit our Web site: **www.group.com**

Credits
Editor: Jim Hawley
Creative Development Editor: Karl Leuthauser
Chief Creative Officer: Joani Schultz
Copy Editor: Betty Taylor
Art Director: Kari K. Monson
Cover Art Director/Designer: Jeff A. Storm
Cover Photographer: Daniel Treat
Print Production Artist: Tracy K. Hindman
Illustrator: Shawn Banner
Production Manager: DeAnne Lear

ISBN 0-7644-2482-3
10 9 8 7 6 5 4 3 2 12 11 10 09 08 07 06

Printed in the United States of America.

Contents

Introduction:
Peer Pressure

"Have a beer! One can't hurt you..."

"Stacy is so stuck up! Now that's she's on the honor roll, she won't even talk to us anymore..."

"So I'm the only one who thinks it's wrong to sneak into *that* movie?..."

"Come on Jenn!" I *need* you to give me the answers so we stay in band together..."

These are just some of the situations preteens find themselves in. The peer pressure that teenagers faced a few years ago is now part of a preteen's everyday world. *Peer Pressure* will help preteens discover how God can help them stand up to the pressure they face in today's world. In the first study, they'll explore negative peer pressure. They will discover ways God can help them respond positively to the pressure from their friends.

The peer pressure that teenagers faced a few years ago is now part of a preteen's everyday world.

Next, preteens will explore an ever-present reality—cliques. They will look at how friendships that close out others are another form of peer pressure, and they'll discover that God wants preteens to be open and accepting of others.

In the third study, your students will explore how to handle pressure from their peers when they face it alone. They will look at how Bible characters faced similar pressure and will discover how God can help them overcome the pressure.

Preteens may feel they can't stand up to the pressure and may give in rather than risking their friendships. The last study will help them see how good decisions go along with good friendships. If a student's friendship leads to trouble, this study will help preteens see this friendship may not be the best one to have.

About Faith 4 Life: Preteen Bible Study Series

The Faith 4 Life: Preteen Bible Study Series helps preteens take a Bible-based approach to faith and life issues. Each book in the series contains these important elements:

• **Life application of Bible truth**—Faith 4 Life studies help preteens understand what the Bible says and then apply that truth to their lives.

• **A relevant topic**—Each Faith 4 Life book focuses on one main topic, with four studies to give your students a thorough understanding of how the Bible relates to that topic.

• **One point**—Each study makes one point, centering on that one theme to make sure students really understand the important truth it conveys. This point is stated upfront and throughout the study.

• **Simplicity**—The studies are easy to use. Each contains a "Before the Study" box that outlines any advance preparation required. Each study also contains a "Study at a Glance" chart so you can quickly and easily see what supplies you'll need and what each study will involve.

• **Action and interaction**—Each study relies on experiential learning to help students learn what God's Word has to say. Preteens discuss and debrief their experiences in large groups, small groups, and individual reflection.

• **Reproducible handouts**—Faith 4 Life books include reproducible handouts for students. No need for student books!

• **Flexible options**—Faith 4 Life preteen studies have two opening and two closing activities. You can choose the options that work best for your students, time frame, or supply needs.

• **Follow-up ideas**—At the end of each book, you'll find a section called "Changed 4 Life." This provides ideas for following up with your students to make sure the Bible truths stick with them.

Use Faith 4 Life studies to show your preteens how the Bible is relevant to their lives. Help them see that God can invade every area of their lives and change them in ways they can only imagine. Encourage your students to go deeper into faith—faith that will sustain them for life! Faith 4 Life, forever!

Handling Negative Peer Pressure

The Point: ➤God wants us to deal positively with negative peer pressure.

Preteens often give in to peer pressure because it's the easy way out. But sometimes kids give in to peer pressure because they can't think of positive ways to resist.

Use this study to help preteens discover positive ways to handle negative peer pressure.

Scripture Source

1 Kings 18:20-38

Elijah tested the prophets of Baal. Under the evil King Ahab's encouragement, the Israelites turned from God and followed the prophets of Baal. Elijah challenged Ahab and his false gods. An altar was set up, and the 450 prophets of Baal called on their god to burn the sacrifice. When nothing happened, Elijah called on God to light his sacrifice. When God sent fire, it not only burned the sacrifice, it destroyed the altar as well.

Romans 12:1-2, 9-10

Paul warns not to conform to the world. He says Christians are to be "living sacrifices," by knowing God and following his will for their lives. He holds up loving and honoring one another as worthy goals.

Philippians 4:8-9

Paul encourages Christians to live to a higher standard—in thoughts and deeds to receive God's peace. Paul uses the example of his life and teachings as a model to practice.

Colossians 3:8-10

Paul teaches Christians to stop living by their earthly natures. He lists several things to avoid—anger, slander, swearing, and lying—which are part of Christians' old selves, because they now have the new nature of Christ living in them.

The Study at a Glance

Section	Minutes	What Students Will Do	Supplies
Warm-Up Option 1	up to 5	**Positive Pressure Charades**—Play a game using positive peer pressure situations.	
Warm-Up Option 2	up to 10	**Pressure Words**—Identify words related to positive and negative peer pressure.	Newsprint, markers, tape
Bible Connection	up to 15	**Conflicting Messages**—Try to form a triangle while blindfolded, then explore the pressure the people faced in 1 Kings 18.	Bibles, blindfolds, newsprint, markers, tape
	up to 15	**Resisting Peer Pressure**—Create skits about peer pressure situations while applying various Scriptural responses.	Bibles
Life Application	up to 10	**Standing Up to Pressure**—Practice identifying signs of negative peer pressure and giving positive responses.	"Pressure Warning Signs" handouts (p. 15), pens
Wrap-Up Option 1	up to 5	**Positive Reflections**—Look at themselves in the mirror and hear why they're special.	Mirror
Wrap-Up Option 2	up to 5	**Uniquely Me**—List what's unique about themselves.	Index cards, pens

Before the Study

Set out Bibles, newsprint, markers, blindfolds, index cards, pens, and a mirror. Also make a photocopy of the "Pressure Warning Signs" handout (p. 15) for each preteen.

The Study

Warm-Up Option 1

Positive Pressure Charades *(up to 5 minutes)*

Have preteens form two groups. **Say: To begin our study today, we're going to play a game of charades. In your groups, think of ways you can demonstrate positive peer pressure with your friends. I'll give groups one minute to think of situations.**

After one minute, have Group 1 present its mime while Group 2 guesses. If Group 2 hasn't guessed in about thirty seconds, have Group 1 reveal its situation. Then have Group 2 present its mime, and give Group 1 thirty seconds to guess. After each group has had a turn, stop the game and

ask:

• Was it hard to come up with positive examples of peer pressure for this game? Why or why not?

• Do you think it would have been easier to use negative examples of peer pressure? Why or why not?

• Which is harder to handle—positive or negative peer pressure? Explain.

Say: Our friends and peers can influence us in many ways. Often that can be a positive thing—such as being active in church or school events. But sometimes the pressure can be negative, encouraging us to do things we know are wrong. Today we're going to explore how ➤God wants us to deal positively with negative peer pressure.

◀ *The Point*

Warm-Up Option 2

Pressure Words *(up to 10 minutes)*

On newsprint, list the following words:

- smoking
- swearing
- lying
- choosing a hairstyle
- taking drugs
- drinking alcohol
- going to church
- getting ears pierced
- shoplifting
- participating in sports
- cheating on tests
- going to movies
- buying designer clothes
- listening to music
- playing computer games
- e-mailing friends
- getting into fights

Tape the newsprint to the wall. Give a marker to each student. Have students each circle words that can result from negative peer pressure or underline ones that can result from positive peer pressure.

Then ask preteens if they agree with each circle or underline. Discuss their responses.

Ask:

• Why are the circled words associated with negative peer pressure?

• Why are the underlined words associated with positive peer pressure?

• Which is harder to handle—positive or negative peer pressure? Explain.

Say: Our friends and peers can influence us in many ways. Often that can

be a positive thing—such as being active in church or school events. But sometimes the pressure can be negative, encouraging us to do things we know are wrong. Today we're going to explore how ➤God wants us to deal positively with negative peer pressure.**

The Point ➤

Bible Connection

Conflicting Messages *(up to 15 minutes)*

Have students form groups of five. If you can't make equal groups, form as many groups of five as you can, and have the remaining kids equally join the other groups. Provide three blindfolds to each group of five, and have group members help blindfold three kids whose birthdays are closest to today's date. Then assign the role of positive pressure to one of the students not wearing a blindfold and negative pressure to the second. You may assign these roles to additional students if your groups have more than five members.

Say: The object of this activity is for blindfolded trios in each group to form a triangle with your bodies. To do this, extend your arms straight out from your sides, like the letter T. Each of you will represent one line of the triangle. Then you will listen to the voices of the remaining kids in your group. When you think you've made the triangle, say "Stop." Then the other members in your group will remove your blindfolds while you keep the triangle shape you've formed.

Tell "positive pressure" people to give good directions to help trios form the triangle. Give "negative pressure" people instructions to disrupt the good directions by giving unhelpful instructions to the trio in their group.

FYI

Whenever groups discuss a list of questions, write the questions on newsprint, and tape the newsprint to the wall so groups can discuss the questions at their own pace.

Allow students a few minutes to try to form their triangles. After this time, stop the activity, and have the other kids remove the blindfolds from the kids in the trios. Allow trios to see how close they've come in forming triangles in this activity. Then have groups discuss the following questions in their groups.

Ask:

- **How did it feel to receive two different kinds of advice on how to form the triangle?**
- **Who did you listen to when trying to form the triangle? Why?**
- **What did you hear that influenced your decisions?**
- **How did listening to the wrong people make your task more difficult?**
- **How did you learn which voices were giving you bad advice?**

Say: In this activity, it wasn't easy to hear the right voice that would help you form your triangle. In real life, either positive or negative things or people can influence you. You may have had a hard time knowing which was which in our triangle activity. But God has given us ways we can know whether the pressure we face from people is positive or negative. Let's explore a story about how God's people faced this problem. I'll set it up for you: Israel was ruled by a bad king named Ahab, and his wife, Jezebel. King Ahab had a man in charge of his palace named Obadiah, who loved the Lord. Now Jezebel did *not* love the Lord. In fact, she was killing all of God's prophets. But Obadiah hid one hundred prophets from Jezebel. While all this was going on, a severe famine occurred. Ahab sent Obadiah to search for food for the animals. While Obadiah was searching, he ran into Elijah, a very important prophet of God. Elijah told Obadiah to arrange a meeting with him and Ahab. Now we can explore the rest of the story.

Form five groups. Assign the five parts of the story to the five groups, 1 Kings 18:16-21, 21-24, 25-29, 30-35, 36-38. Give each group newsprint and markers. Allow each group to draw the scene revealed in its assigned verses. Allow about five minutes for groups to complete their drawings. Then have groups present their drawings in order. Tape up newsprint sheets in story order as groups present. After the story,

ask:

- **What kind of pressure did the people face?**
- **Why do you think the people followed Baal instead of God?**
- **How is the peer pressure you face like or unlike the pressure the people faced in our story?**

Say: The people in this story were pressured by their king and queen to worship false Gods. It was so bad, God's prophets were being killed off by Jezebel! You probably won't face that kind of pressure, but when friends or others pressure you into doing what you know is wrong, it's a serious issue. ➤God wants us to deal positively with negative peer pressure. Let's look at some Bible verses that can help you face this pressure.

◀ ***The Point***

Resisting Peer Pressure *(up to 15 minutes)*

Form groups of up to four. Provide Bibles, and have volunteers in each group read the following passages aloud to their group members: Romans 12:1-2, 9-10;

Philippians 4:8-9; and Colossians 3:8-10. Have each group choose a situation in which they face some type of peer pressure. For example, groups could create a skit in which someone is pressured to take drugs or is being teased for not having the latest clothes. Then have kids create a simple skit. After a few minutes of preparing the skits, have groups present their skits twice—first giving in to the peer pressure, and the second time applying the principles they've discovered in the Bible passages to resist the pressure. Following the skits,

ask:

• How can these Scriptures you applied to your skits help you overcome peer pressure?

• What are some pressures students your age are facing now?

Say: Let's explore some possible pressures you're facing now and see how God can help you ➤deal positively with negative peer pressure.

The Point ➤

Life Application

Standing Up to Pressure *(up to 10 minutes)*

Form groups of up to four. Distribute the "Pressure Warning Signs" handouts (p. 15) and pens. **Say: This handout has some possible negative peer-pressure situations you may find yourselves in. Talk about the situations in your groups, and describe the warning signs of the peer-pressure situations listed. Then list some positive responses to the negative pressure. You'll find a blank section to fill in your own example of pressure you may be facing.**

Allow groups a few minutes to complete the handouts. Then have groups discuss them.

Ask:

• What are the most common warning signs of negative peer pressure?

• Why is it often difficult to say no to friends even though you think you should?

• How will you respond to these pressures when they come up again?

Say: Peer pressure can be a powerful force. But God is a greater force, and he can help you ➤deal positively with negative peer pressure. Let's close with one more way we can overcome negative peer pressure.

The Point ➤

Wrap-Up Option 1

Positive Reflections *(up to 5 minutes)*

Have preteens form a circle.

Say: One of the best ways to overcome negative peer pressure is to recognize how special you are in God's eyes. Even though you're pressured to be the same as everyone else, you're each unique.

Go around the circle while holding a mirror in front of you. As you stand by each person, put the mirror in front of his or her face and **say:** [Name], **I thank God for you because...**

Affirm each student by saying something unique about him or her. Then have one or two preteens say why they're thankful for that person. Keep things moving quickly by allowing only two or three positive phrases about each person as you go around the circle. Close with prayer, thanking God for the unique qualities of each person in the class.

Wrap-Up Option 2

Uniquely Me *(up to 5 minutes)*

Give each preteen an index card and a pen. **Say: One of the best ways to fight peer pressure is to recognize how special you are in God's eyes. You don't have to do what everyone else is doing, because God didn't make you like them.**

Have preteens write three unique things about themselves on their index cards. Suggest they include such things as their favorite hobbies, favorite foods, and special qualities or abilities they have. Then have kids pass their cards to you. Challenge kids to guess who wrote each card as you read it. One by one, read the cards.

Say: Even though you're pressured to be the same as everyone else, you're each unique.

Close the lesson with prayer, thanking God for making each person unique.

Extra-Time Tips

Use these extra ideas to add some creative fun to your studies. They are low-prep or no-prep ideas that work in no time!

True Stories—Form groups of three. Have group members each tell about one time when friends pressured them to do something they felt was wrong (without mentioning names). Have group members tell how they responded and why.

Pressure Support Cards—Give preteens an index card and a pen. Have them form pairs. Have each person write a brief note of encouragement to fight negative peer pressure and give it to his or her partner.

Pressure Warning Signs

Read the statements below. For each statement, write why it is negative peer pressure. Then write how you would respond to the pressure.

WHAT FRIENDS SAY…	WARNING SIGNS	MY RESPONSES
You don't want to be seen with her. She's a Christian.	*Friends are telling me what to do—deciding who should be my friends.*	*I know. What's wrong with being a Christian?*
Don't worry about that math test. Just have a beer and forget it!		
Drugs make you feel good. They can't hurt you if you only do them once in a while. Here, take a hit on this.		
We can get into R-rated movies. We do it all the time. You comin' or are you wimpin' out?		
We're going to knock that new kid's books all over the hallway. This'll be fun. Come on, we need your help.		
Write your own pressure situation here:		

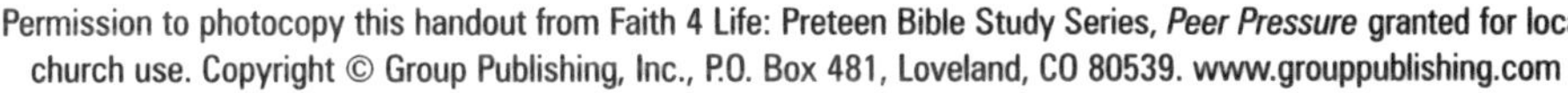

Accepting Others

The Point: ➤ God wants us to accept others.

Close friendships are good for preteens. A circle of friends offers acceptance, people to do things with, and people to identify with. But when circles of friends shut out others, they become cliques.

Use this study to help preteens develop open friendships as they learn how to be more accepting of others.

Scripture Source

Mark 2:13-17

Jesus dined with Levi and other tax collectors. While Jesus was in Levi's house, the guests included tax collectors and "sinners," according to the Pharisees' description. Jesus responded to the Pharisees' critique by saying he had come for sinners, not the righteous.

Luke 7:36-50

Jesus dined with the Pharisees. While dining, a woman who had "lived a sinful life" came to Jesus, poured perfume on him, and washed his feet with her tears. In response to the Pharisees' disapproval, Jesus told a simple parable and directed it at the response of the Pharisee Simon. The parable was about two people—one with a large debt and the other with a small debt—forgiven by the same creditor. Jesus asked which person would be more grateful. Jesus applied the parable to the woman, who was forgiven the large debt. This was in contrast to Simon the Pharisee having the lesser debt.

Luke 19:1-10

Jesus told Zacchaeus he would stay with him. Zacchaeus was a short man and a tax collector who climbed a tree to see Jesus. In Jesus' time, tax collectors were considered among the most despised people because they charged their fellow Jews exorbitant taxes under the protection of the hated Roman rulers. When Jesus saw his effort, he told Zacchaeus he must stay with him. Zacchaeus joyfully told Jesus he would give half his possessions to the poor and pay back four times anyone he had cheated.

John 4:4-10

Jesus talked with a Samaritan woman. The Jews' hatred for the Samaritans was based primarily on history and race. Samaritans were descendants of a mix of Israelites and the natives of Palestine. By talking with her, Jesus showed his disciples he cares for all people.

The Study at a Glance

Section	Minutes	What Students Will Do	Supplies
Warm-Up Option 1	up to 10	**Balloon Cliques**—Form groups that represent cliques.	Balloons, permanent markers, paper, pens
Warm-Up Option 2	up to 10	**Different Circles**—Identify and mime cliques from school.	Newsprint, marker, tape
Bible Connection	up to 15	**Closed Circles**—Exclude others from joining their cliques, then compare activity to Mark 2:13-17.	Bible, newsprint, marker, tape
	up to 15	**Jesus Accepts All**—Research examples of Jesus' acceptance of people and create skits of the events.	Bibles
Life Application	up to 10	**A Look at Myself**—Complete handouts about how they relate to others.	"Open and Closed Circles" handouts (p. 25), pens
Wrap-Up Option 1	up to 10	**Balloon Friends**—Demonstrate how all students are important by opening up a balloon-person clique.	Balloons from Warm-Up Option 1 "Balloon Cliques" activity, string, scissors
Wrap-Up Option 2	up to 5	**Open Circles**—Affirm that they're each important by signing handouts.	"Open and Closed Circles" handouts (used previously), pens

Before the Study

Set out Bibles, balloons, permanent markers, newsprint, paper, pens, string, and scissors. Also make a photocopy of the "Open and Closed Circles" handout (p. 25) for each preteen.

The Study

Warm-Up Option 1

Balloon Cliques *(up to 10 minutes)*

Provide a balloon and a permanent marker to each student. Have each student blow up the balloon and draw either a large diamond, a triangle, or a circle on the balloon, without letting the other students see which shape he or she has drawn. Then have each student draw a face in the shape. Designate different corners of the room for each of the three groups: Diamondheads, Triheads, and Circleheads. Then have students stand in the appropriate sections of the room according to the shapes of their balloon. Provide paper and pens to groups.

Say: We've just formed three groups of people—the Diamondheads, the Triheads, and the Circleheads. Now, as a group, agree on five things your little group of friends is known for. For example, you might say your group listens exclusively to one type of music or wears a certain style of clothes.

Allow groups a few minutes to record five characteristics of their groups. Then have each group choose a volunteer to share the group's five things.

Ask:

- **Is there a group you'd rather be in based on what it's known for? Why or why not?**
- **What's a clique?**
- **How are these groups of balloon people like cliques?**

Say: It's normal to be attracted to people who have the same interests or abilities you have. If you play a musical instrument or enjoy hoops, you want to join other people who do the same. The problem comes when the group becomes cliquish and excludes other people or thinks its group is better than another. We've been exploring peer pressure, and today we're going to look into cliques. We'll see how this problem isn't new and discover how ➤God wants us to accept others. ◄ The Point

Have kids save their balloon people if you've chosen Wrap-Up Option 1.

Warm-Up Option 2

Different Circles *(up to 10 minutes)*

Form groups of up to four. **Say: In school, you see many different groups of people who always spend time together.**

Ask:

- **What's a clique?**
- **What are some of the cliques or groups at your school?**

While students share, write their responses on a piece of newsprint.

Say: Each group should choose one group from this list and prepare a thirty-second mime of how that group might worship at church.

Coordinate the groups so they don't all choose the same clique to mime. Allow a few minutes for groups to prepare their mimes. Then have each group present its mime to the larger group. Have students guess which clique is being mimed.

Ask:

- **What's unique about each group that was mimed?**
- **What makes people want to spend time together?**
- **How do you feel when the group you're in is called a clique?**
- **Are cliques always bad? Explain.**

The Point ➤

Say: It's normal to be attracted to people who have the same interests or abilities you have. If you play a musical instrument or enjoy hoops, you want to join other people who do the same. The problem comes when the group becomes cliquish and excludes other people or thinks its group is better than another. We've been exploring peer pressure, and today we're going to look into cliques. We'll see how this problem isn't new and discover how ➤God wants us to accept others.

Bible Connection

Closed Circles *(up to 15 minutes)*

Ask for two or three volunteers. Have them go outside the room, and then form groups of two to six with the remaining students.

Tell kids to pretend their groups are cliques. Tell each group to form a tight circle, facing inward. Have kids begin talking within their cliques about a subject of their choice. Instruct the groups to exclude the "outsiders" from their conversations and physically move as needed to keep them out of their circle.

Bring the outsiders back in, and ask them to join any group's conversation they want. After two minutes, stop the exercise and form a circle.

Direct the next two questions to the outsiders.

Ask:

- **Was it easy to get into the circles? Explain.**
- **What actions or words did you use to try to get in?**

Then direct the next two questions to the rest of the students.

Ask:

- **Was it easy to keep the outsiders out? Explain.**
- **How is this exercise similar to real-life situations?**

Write the following incomplete sentences on a sheet of newsprint, and tape it to a wall.

- I tried to get into a group of friends by...
- We tried to keep someone out of our group by...
- When I was excluded from a group or groups, I felt...
- Leaving someone out of our group made me feel...
- When I realized I couldn't get into a group, I...

Then ask preteens to complete the sentences verbally based on the exercise and real-life experiences. On the newsprint, write several of their responses to each sentence. Discuss the endings written on the newsprint.

Say: The problem of being excluded from a group is not a new one.

Have a volunteer read aloud Mark 2:13-17.

Ask:

- **How did Jesus treat the people in this passage?**
- **How did the various people in this passage respond to Jesus?**
- **How does this situation compare with times you've been excluded from a group?**

Say: People are excluded for different reasons. Let's explore some more Bible examples as we look deeper into how ➤ God wants us to accept others.

◀ *The Point*

Jesus Accepts All *(up to 15 minutes)*

Have preteens form three groups. Assign one of the following passages to each group: Luke 7:36-50; 19:1-10; and John 4:4-10. **Say: Each group has a Bible passage in which Jesus interacted with a person who was excluded for a certain**

FYI

When you ask for volunteers to exclude from the larger group, be sensitive to how a student might react to this role. It may be best to select from preteens who don't feel left out in real life. Also, be aware of how students may respond during debriefing times for this and other activities in this study. Make a point to connect with any students who show they are more likely to be left out of cliques or groups.

reason. Each group should research its passage to determine why the person was excluded. Then create a short skit to re-create the Bible event for the class.

Allow about five minutes for groups to research their passages and create their skits. Then have groups share their research findings and present their skits. Following the last group presentation, have groups gather together.

Ask:

- **How is the situation in your passage like situations in your life?**
- **By his actions and words, what does Jesus say about cliques?**
- **What reassurance does Jesus give to the outsiders in these passages?**
- **How can that reassurance help us?**

The Point ➤

Say: It is clear from his actions ➤Jesus wants us to accept others. Let's see how well we're doing this.

Life Application

A Look at Myself *(up to 10 minutes)*

Say: How well do you relate to other people? Think about how you relate to others and whether you encourage open or closed circles of friends.

Give each student an "Open and Closed Circles" handout (p. 25) and a pen.

Have preteens answer all the questions and score themselves according to the directions at the bottom of the handout. Encourage them each to choose one area they do well in and one they would like to improve in. Form new groups of three, and have them talk about their choices.

FYI

Whenever groups discuss a list of questions, write the questions on newsprint, and tape the newsprint to the wall so groups can discuss the questions at their own pace.

Ask:

- **Is it easy to encourage open circles? Why or why not?**
- **How can the examples of Jesus that we explored help us be more open?**
- **Are there some people you should leave out of your circles? Explain.**
- **Based on your handout results, in what area can you improve in the next few weeks?**

Say: We've seen that we all can improve in including people. We have Jesus' example as the greatest motivation for being more open. Let's commit to do that.

Wrap-Up Option 1

Balloon Friends *(up to 10 minutes)*

Choose this option if you opened with the Option 1 "Balloon Cliques" activity. Re-form the groups from the "Balloon Cliques" activity. Cut string into three six-foot lengths, and give each group a six-foot length of string. **Say: Form a string circle on the floor, and place all your balloon people in it.**

Pause while students do this. **Say: You've just formed three cliques. Now, using all three strings, form one large circle, and place the balloon people in it.**

Ask:

- **How is this still a clique? What can you change to make it an open circle?**

Have a volunteer change the string circle to make it an open circle. The volunteer might move the string so it's shaped more like a C than a circle. Then have students hold hands and form a circle with you.

As you say the following, release one of your hands to symbolize opening your circle. **Say: We're all important people in this circle of friends. Let's try to be more like Jesus and keep our circle open to new people, too.**

Have preteens form pairs. Have partners pray for each other, asking God for help in reaching out to people and for strength in overcoming pressures to exclude others.

Wrap-Up Option 2

Open Circles *(up to 5 minutes)*

Say: To symbolize that each of us is included in an open circle, I want each person to sign his or her name on the back of everyone's "Open and Closed Circles" handout.

Encourage preteens to contact new or inactive members of the church and invite them to your activities.

Close with a group prayer, and then say: **"A new command I give you: Love one another. As I have loved you, so you must love one another"** (John 13:34).

Extra-Time Tips

Use these extra ideas to add some creative fun to your studies. They are low-prep or no-prep ideas that work in no time!

Inclusiveness Practice—Form groups of up to four. Have each group choose a clique and practice role playing the clique's characters. Then have preteens mingle with other groups—while in character—and practice, with their words and actions, including others in their circle of friends. Afterward,

ask:

- **Was it easy to include others? Why or why not?**
- **What did you say and do to include others?**
- **How can people with different interests open up to one another?**

"Open Circle" Words—Vertically down the middle of a piece of paper, have preteens write, "Open Circle." Then have them use the letters to write words or phrases that would remind them of how to have open circles of friends. For example:

Open up to strangers
be **P**olite
show **E**nthusiasm for others
Never look down on others

Form pairs, and have partners share their word creations with each other.

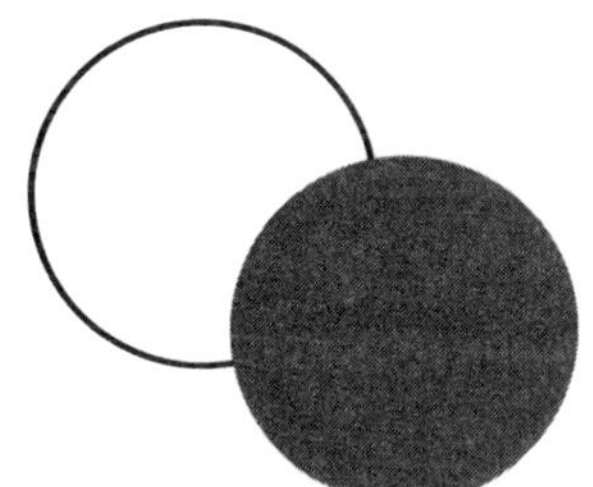

Open and Closed Circles

This questionnaire will help you think about whether you and your friends tend to form open or closed circles. Answer the questions as honestly as possible. Check "often," "sometimes," or "rarely" for each one.

	OFTEN	SOMETIMES	RARELY
1. All my friends and I spend time together doing the same things.	❍	❍	❍
2. I spend time with many different friends.	❍	❍	❍
3. My friends and I all dress alike.	❍	❍	❍
4. When I'm with a group of people, I look for people who seem lonely and try to make friends with them.	❍	❍	❍
5. When I see a new person being included in my circle of friends, I feel jealous.	❍	❍	❍
6. I tend to do different activities with different people.	❍	❍	❍
7. I'm embarrassed if my friends see me with someone they think is a nerd.	❍	❍	❍
8. I appreciate the different interests and hobbies my friends have, even when they aren't what I like.	❍	❍	❍
9. I'm most comfortable doing things with the same people all the time.	❍	❍	❍
10. I like to get to know new people.	❍	❍	❍
11. I'm careful about who I introduce to my friends.	❍	❍	❍
12. I go out of my way to make a new person feel welcome in my circle of friends.	❍	❍	❍

Scoring

For each question you answered "sometimes," give yourself one point. _____

For each odd-numbered question you answered "rarely," give yourself two points. _____

For each even-numbered question you answered "often," give yourself two points. _____

Total: _____

19 to 24 points: You tend to include others in your circle of friends. Keep it up!
9 to 18 points: Although you can reach out, you sometimes exclude others—perhaps without knowing it. Work on including new friends.
0 to 8 points: You tend to belong to a closed circle of friends. Concentrate on reaching out to new people and developing friendships outside your group.

Study 3

You're Not Alone

The Point: ➤God can help us face peer pressure when we're alone.

Friends often pressure preteens to do things they don't want to do. But when only one tries to stand up to the crowd, it's tough to say no. Kids may not feel secure in their ability to withstand negative peer pressure when they face it alone.

Use this study to help preteens learn to know and trust God and their worth in God's eyes, to singularly overcome the pressure from others they face.

Scripture Source

Psalm 100:3

The psalmist praises God for making us and caring for us, because we are the sheep of God's pasture.

Matthew 26:69-75

Peter denied Jesus three times. After Jesus' arrest, Peter and the other disciples fled. Peter was outside of where Jesus' was being held, and Peter denied knowing or being with Jesus to three different people. He even called down curses on himself the third time.

Ephesians 6:10-18

Paul tells the church to put on God's armor. Although this letter was addressed to the Ephesian church, its message was intended for Christians in the general area of Asia. Using armor language, Paul describes the spiritual armor Christians have for fighting worldliness.

The Study at a Glance

Section	Minutes	What Students Will Do	Supplies
Warm-Up Option 1	up to 10	**Buying Pressure**—Spend fake money and see how other people influence their buying choices.	"Funny Money" sheet (pp. 34-35), store catalogs, product advertisements from newspapers, scissors, paper, pens
Warm-Up Option 2	up to 10	**Pressure Travel**—Try to influence another's dream travel plans.	
Bible Connection	up to 15	**All By Myself**—Experience going against the crowd, then explore Peter's denial of Christ.	Bibles, paper, pens
	up to 15	**Alone But *Not* Alone**—Draw pressure situations and illustrate how the armor of Ephesians 6 helps them face those situations.	Bibles, newsprint, markers
Life Application	up to 10	**Approval Temperature—R**eflect on Psalm 100:3 and evaluate how well they handle peer pressure.	Bible, "Approval Thermometer" handouts (p. 36), markers
Wrap-Up Option 1	up to 10	**Peer Encouragement**—Write encouraging notes to one another.	Index cards, envelopes, pens, tape
Wrap-Up Option 2	up to 5	**Positive Pressure**—Give and receive encouraging words.	

Before the Study

Set out Bibles, store catalogs and product advertisements from newspapers, pens, paper, scissors, newsprint, markers, envelopes, and index cards. Also make photocopies of the "Funny Money" sheets (pp. 34-35) and the "Approval Thermometer" handout (p. 36) for each preteen.

The Study

Warm-Up Option 1

Buying Pressure *(up to 10 minutes)*

Give each preteen $50 and $100 "Funny Money" sheets (pp. 34-35) and a pair of scissors. Have kids cut out the bills while you explain the activity. **Say: You get to decide if you'll buy the items listed in the catalogs and ads. You each have nine hundred dollars in funny money to use to purchase the items you want. You can talk to one another about your choices and decisions.**

Place paper, pens, catalogs, and store ads on a table, and ask students to quickly look through them to decide how they'll "spend" their money. Have preteens each write on a piece of paper what they choose to buy before giving you the money. Then have them give you the money they've spent. After everyone has spent all his or her money, have students compare lists.

Ask:

• **Were you influenced to buy things other people were buying? Why or why not?**

• **If you had real money to buy these things, would you be influenced differently? Explain.**

• **How do others influence you in real life?**

Say: Your peers may have influenced you to buy things in this activity. And your peers may influence you in other ways as well. But how you respond to peer pressure when you don't have your friends around may be a different story. Today we're going to explore that situation and discover how ➤God can help us face peer pressure when we're alone.

◀ *The Point*

Warm-Up Option 2

Pressure Travel *(up to 10 minutes)*

Form groups of four to six. Ask for a volunteer from each group. Tell the volunteers to think about where they'd go and what they'd do if they could travel anywhere they wanted. Send the volunteers outside the room. Then tell the rest of the students to try to influence the volunteers' decisions.

Invite the volunteers back in, and **say: Take two minutes to talk with your group about where you want to go. If you aren't sure, ask for suggestions.** Afterward, have the volunteers answer the following question.

Ask:

• **Were your travel plans influenced by what the rest of your group said? Why or why not?**

Then **ask** everyone:

• **How do your friends influence what you do in real life?**

Say: Your peers may have influenced you to change your plans in this activity. And your peers may influence you in other ways as well. But how you respond to peer pressure when you don't have your friends around may be a different story. Today we're going to explore that situation and discover how

The Point ➤ ➤**God can help us face peer pressure when we're alone.**

Bible Connection

All By Myself *(up to 15 minutes)*

Say: Now that we've seen how others can influence our decisions, we'll experience how difficult it can be to stand up against peer pressure when we're all alone.

Have a volunteer stand on the outside of a closed door that opens in. Have everyone else stand on the other side of the door. Tell the volunteer to try to enter the room. Tell the rest of the students to hold the door closed and not let the volunteer in. If the volunteer can't open the door, call time. Then have the group stand four feet away from the door. Tell kids to try to convince the volunteer to stay out by calling out reasons not to open the door. Have the volunteer try once again to enter the room. After he or she gets into the room, form a circle.

Ask the volunteer:

- **How was trying to enter the room the first time like trying to beat peer pressure when you're alone?**
- **How much easier was entering the room when there was more distance between you and the rest of the kids?**

Then **ask** the other students:

- **How can you put distance between you and the pressures you face?**
- **What can help you when your friends aren't around?**

Say: When your friends aren't around to encourage you, it's often harder to stand up to the pressure.

Ask a few volunteers to read Matthew 26:69-75. **Say: I want each of you to imagine you are Peter after this event.**

Provide paper and pens, and have each student find a place by him or herself. Have students spend a few minutes writing journal entries as if they were Peter. Then have preteens form pairs and share their journal entries with their partners. Have pairs discuss the following questions with their partner.

Ask:

- **What was it like to write as if you were Peter?**
- **What difficult situation have you faced when you were alone?**

Say: Peter spent three years with Jesus and the other disciples. But when he faced a crisis and he was alone, he denied Jesus. We don't have to make the same mistake when we're alone. ➤God can help us face peer pressure when we're alone. Let's see how.

◀ *The Point*

Alone But *Not* Alone *(up to 15 minutes)*

Say: Even when your friends aren't with you, you aren't alone to fight peer pressure. Let's explore a Bible passage that shows us how God's Word will give us what we need to withstand peer pressure.

Have preteens form groups of up to four. Provide Bibles, newsprint, and markers. Have a volunteer in each group read aloud Ephesians 6:10-18 to the other group members. Then have group members draw situations in which the "armor" described in this passage can help them face pressure when they're alone. For example, kids might draw a shield between themselves and a group of kids offering a cigarette.

FYI

Whenever groups discuss a list of questions, write the questions on newsprint, and tape the newsprint to the wall so groups can discuss the questions at their own pace.

Allow about five minutes for groups to complete their drawings. Then have groups present their pictures and explain them to the larger group. Have groups discuss the following questions in their groups.

Ask:

- **How do you feel when you're alone and faced with peer pressure?**
- **What part of God's armor is most helpful for you? Explain.**
- **In what situations do you need God's help against negative pressure when you're alone?**

Say: ➤God can help us face peer pressure when we're alone. We've seen how God's armor is one way he helps us. Let's explore another way.

◀ *The Point*

Life Application

Approval Temperature *(up to 10 minutes)*

Give an "Approval Thermometer" handout (p. 36) and a marker to each student. **Say: Many people give in to peer pressure because they don't feel confident or good about themselves. If you feel good about yourself, you won't be as easily influenced by the negative things others want you to do.**

Have preteens read the statements next to the thermometer, from bottom to top, and each make a mark when they reach a statement that's not true for them.

Then have them color their thermometers up to that statement.

Say: **The higher you've marked your temperature, the more likely you are to rely on others for approval. And that makes you more vulnerable to peer pressure.**

Have a volunteer read aloud Psalm 100:3.

Ask:

• **Knowing that God made each of us, how does that affect the way you see yourself?**

Say: **God made us and cares for us. The next time you're alone and face pressure to do wrong, remember this verse and the truths we've learned today.**

Wrap-Up Option 1

Peer Encouragement *(up to 10 minutes)*

Give each student the same number of index cards as you have students, up to ten cards. Also provide envelopes and pens to students. Say: **Biblical truths and God's own acknowledgment of our worth help us feel good about ourselves. But it's important to hear encouragement from our peers too. ➤God can help us face peer pressure when we're alone. By writing encouraging words to one another, we can be strengthened when we're alone.**

The Point ➤

Have students write their names on their envelopes. Write your name on one too. Tape the envelopes to the walls around the room. Then join the preteens in writing brief notes of encouragement to one another to stand up to peer pressure. Write the notes on the index cards, and place them in the appropriate envelopes. Have students seal their envelopes and take them home to read.

Close with a prayer, asking for God's help and strength to fight negative peer pressure.

Wrap-Up Option 2

Positive Pressure *(up to 5 minutes)*

Say: **Biblical truths and God's own acknowledgment of our worth help us feel good about ourselves. But it's important to hear encouragement from our peers too. ➤God can help us face peer pressure when we're alone. Hearing encouraging words makes it easier to overcome negative peer pressure when we're alone.**

The Point ➤

Form a circle, and have one person stand in the middle. Tell students to call out to the person in the center words of encouragement to stand up to peer pressure. Then have the next person step into the center. Keep things moving by allowing only three or four comments for each person. Realize some preteens may feel uncomfortable giving or receiving compliments, so encourage them to give it a try. Remind students to be positive. Be sure to include yourself in this activity.

Close by praying for God's help and strength to fight negative peer pressure.

Extra-Time Tips

Use these extra ideas to add some creative fun to your studies. They are low-prep or no-prep ideas that work in no time!

Putting On the Armor—Form groups of up to five. Have each group plan and perform a skit that demonstrates how someone can stand up to peer pressure when he or she is alone.

I'm Not Alone Cards—Give preteens a credit-card-size piece of paper or card stock. On one side, have students write, "When others pressure me, I'm not alone." Then have them pass their cards around so each person can sign the backs. Ask students to keep their cards in their wallets or purses.

FUNNY MONEY

100
ONE HUNDRED
FUNNY MONEY
31906572 G
12
319065
L
FAKER'S RESERVE NOTE

FUNNY MONEY

50
FIFTY
FUNNY MONEY

50
FIFTY
FUNNY MONEY

50
FIFTY
FUNNY MONEY

50
FIFTY
FUNNY MONEY

50
FIFTY
FUNNY MONEY

50
FIFTY
FUNNY MONEY

APPROVAL THERMOMETER

I'm willing to do anything to be liked.

I want friends' approval for my actions.

I want everyone to like me.

I want friends' approval for my clothing.

I want my best friends to like me.

I like myself.

Study 4

Good Decisions and Good Friendships

The Point: ➤ God can help us keep our true friends and help us make good decisions.

Preteens who stand up to their friends may risk losing friendships. Sometimes that risk may seem too high a price to pay, and kids may give in to the pressure.

Use this study to help preteens make good decisions and still maintain healthy friendships.

Scripture Source

Genesis 13:5-12

Abram and Lot separated. Abram's and Lot's herdsmen argued, and Abram suggested to Lot that they separate so they would not bring trouble on their respective families or let their enemies see their conflict. Abram gave Lot the choice of which direction to settle, and they both settled in different areas.

1 Samuel 25:2-17, 23-25

Nabal was a wealthy landowner who was evil and foolish. When David's men asked for provisions as they traveled through Nabal's land, Nabal insulted them. While David prepared to attack, Nabal's wife, Abigail, rushed ahead to meet David and take the blame on herself.

Acts 5:1-11

Ananias sold his property and, with his wife's knowledge, lied about the price to the apostles. Peter confronted Ananias and condemned him for lying. Ananias died at that moment. Later Sapphira, not knowing Ananias' fate, also told Peter the same lie, and she too fell down dead.

Acts 15:36-41

Paul and Barnabas disagreed over who to take with them on a missionary journey. Paul didn't want to take John Mark, but Barnabas did. They agreed to part company; Barnabas took John Mark, and Paul chose Silas to accompany him on the journey.

James 3:13-18

James contrasted two types of wisdom. He stated that good deeds and humility are examples of Godly wisdom, whereas envy, pride, and selfishness characterize earthly wisdom.

The Study at a Glance

Section	Minutes	What Students Will Do	Supplies
Warm-Up Option 1	up to 10	**Odd Square Out**—Draw shapes on newsprint to demonstrate going against the crowd.	Newsprint, markers, tape
Warm-Up Option 2	up to 10	**Follow the Beat**—Clap at different beats to demonstrate being different.	
Bible Connection	up to 15	**Peer Pressure Advice**—Choose good and bad possibilities for various Bible situations.	Bibles, index cards, pens
	up to 15	**Choose Your Advice**—Make choices based on advice from group members, then create wisdom phrases based on James 13:13-18.	Bibles, index cards from "Peer Pressure Advice" activity, envelopes, index cards, pens
Life Application	up to 10	**Friendly Pressure**—Practice ways of saying no to friends who pressure them.	"Positive Pressure" handouts (p. 44)
Wrap-Up Option 1	up to 5	**Square Prayers**—Write and cut out newsprint prayers.	Newsprint from Warm-Up Option 1 "Odd Square Out" activity, markers
Wrap-Up Option 2	up to 5	**Unison Prayers**—Write and say prayers in unison.	Paper, pens

Before the Study

Set out Bibles, newsprint, markers, index cards, paper, pens, and tape. Also make a photocopy of the "Positive Pressure" handout (p. 44) for each preteen.

The Study

Warm-Up Option 1

Odd Square Out *(up to 10 minutes)*

Tape several sheets of newsprint to a wall. You'll need about a five-foot-long piece for every three students. Provide a marker to each student. Ask for one volunteer, and tell him or her to draw squares while you ask everyone else to draw circles. **Say: Each of you will have two minutes to draw circles about the size of your fist. Everyone must draw circles, and the circles cannot touch one another. We'll draw until the newsprint is filled or until two minutes are up.**

Begin the activity. Direct the volunteer to move to the different sheets of newsprint and draw his or her squares. After two minutes or when the newsprint is filled, call time.

Ask the volunteer:

- **How did you feel as the only person drawing squares?**

Direct the following questions to everyone.

Ask:

- **Which shape stands out on the newsprint? Why?**
- **Do you ever feel like a square in the middle of your "circle" of peers? Why or why not?**
- **When friends pressure you to do wrong, how hard is it to stand up to them? Explain.**
- **How is standing up to friends' pressure like drawing squares while everyone else is drawing circles?**

Say: There are times when friends pressure you into making bad choices. Although you want to keep your friends, you also want to do what you know is right. ➤God can help us keep our true friends and help us make good decisions. Let's discover how.

◀ *The Point*

Warm-Up Option 2

Follow the Beat *(up to 10 minutes)*

Ask for a volunteer, and have the other students form a circle around the volunteer. Have kids begin clapping in unison to a steady beat. Then have the volunteer clap to a different beat. Give a few more volunteers turns in the center of the circle.

Ask the volunteers:

- **How easy was it to clap to a different beat?**

Direct the following questions to everyone.

Ask:

- **Which beat was easier to hear? Why?**
- **Do you ever feel as if you're clapping to a different beat? Why or why not?**

• **When friends pressure you to do wrong, how hard is it to stand up to them? Explain.**

• **How is standing up to friends' pressure like clapping to a different beat?**

Say: There are times when friends pressure you into making bad choices. Although you want to keep your friends, you also want to do what you know is right. ➤God can help us keep our true friends and help us make good decisions. Let's discover how.

The Point ➤

Bible Connection

Peer Pressure Advice *(up to 15 minutes)*

Have preteens form four groups. Provide Bibles, index cards, and pens. Assign one of the following passages to each group: Genesis 13:5-7; 1 Samuel 25:2-11; Acts 5:1-6; and Acts 15:36-38.

Say: Sometimes advice from your friends or other people is good, and other times it's not so good. In your groups, choose two good responses and two bad responses to the problems revealed in your Bible passages. Write each response on an index card.

FYI

Whenever groups discuss a list of questions, write the questions on newsprint, and tape the newsprint to the wall so groups can discuss the questions at their own pace.

Allow a few minutes for groups to work. Then have a volunteer from each group summarize the Bible story and share his or her group's four index card responses. After the last group has shared, have groups discuss the following questions.

Ask:

• **Were the positive or negative responses easier to come up with for your Bible situations? Explain.**

• **If you were in your group's Bible situation, how would you respond?**

• **How were these situations similar to pressure you've faced? different?**

Say: Let's see how the people did respond in your Bible situations.

Provide the following passages to the appropriate groups: Genesis 13:8-12; 1 Samuel 25:12-17, 23-25; Acts 5:5-11; and Acts 15:39-41. Allow groups a few minutes to discover the endings of their Bible situations. Then allow groups to share the Bible event outcomes with the class. Have groups discuss the following questions:

Ask:

• **Did the people or person who had to make a decision in the Bible story make a good one? Explain.**

• **What can you learn about making good decisions from this Bible situation?**

Say: The Bible situations had both good and bad outcomes. Sometimes we may be tempted to give in to bad decisions because we like our friends. But ➤God can help us keep our true friends and help us make good decisions. Let's examine some wisdom from the Bible to help us do this.

◄ *The Point*

Choose Your Advice *(up to 15 minutes)*

Choose two index cards with bad advice and two with good advice from the "Peer Pressure Advice" activity, and place them in separate envelopes. Number the envelopes from one to four, and place them on the floor or table so the numbers are visible.

Form three groups. Ask for a volunteer from each group to be a contestant. Explain that the object is to end up with an envelope that contains good advice. Tell each contestant's group members that their job is to shout instructions to their contestant.

Have contestants each choose an envelope. Then give each contestant an opportunity to trade his or her envelope with another contestant, or exchange the envelope with one still on the table.

Then have contestants in turn open their envelopes and read their advice. Tell teammates to cheer if their advice is good and boo if it's bad.

Ask the contestants:

- **How did it feel to choose an envelope?**
- **Who made the final decision on which envelope to choose—you or your group members? Why?**
- **How did you feel when you found you made the right or wrong decision?**

Ask everyone:

- **How much influence did group members have on their contestants?**
- **How was your group's influence like the influence friends have when you make decisions?**
- **Who lives with the consequences of the decisions?**

Say: In this game, you made choices by guessing or listening to your group members. But in real life, you have God's Word to guide you.

Have preteens form groups of up to four, and provide Bibles, index cards, and pens for each group. Have a volunteer in each group read aloud James 3:13-18. Then, based on the Bible passage, have group members write "wisdom phrases" for countering peer pressure. For example, groups could write, "If my friends want me to lie, the Bible says this isn't wisdom to live by."

After groups have created at least three wisdom phrases, have each group share one phrase with the class. **Say: This activity has shown us how ➤God can help us keep our true friends and help us make good decisions. Next we'll practice some ways to say no to pressure while keeping our friends.**

The Point ➤

Life Application

Friendly Pressure *(up to 10 minutes)*

Form groups of up to five. Distribute the "Positive Pressure" handouts (p. 44). Have groups follow the instructions on the handout and practice the "saying no" techniques.

Ask:

- **Which response is most comfortable for you to use? least? Explain.**
- **Which responses would probably work best in most situations? Explain.**
- **Which responses can you use in the coming week to say no to negative peer pressure?**

Say: Take your handout with you to help you know positive ways to resist pressure from your friends.

Wrap-Up Option 1

Square Prayers *(up to 5 minutes)*

Use this option if you chose the Warm-Up Option 1 "Odd Square Out" activity.

Say: Sometimes it isn't easy to make good decisions when friends disagree with you. ➤God can help us keep our true friends and help us make good decisions. Let's write prayers about this.

The Point ➤

Give a marker to each student. Have students each write a short prayer in one of the boxes on the newsprint from the "Odd Square Out" activity. Then have kids tear out the square prayers. Shuffle them and give one to each preteen.

Form a circle. Have each student read aloud his or her square prayer, then hand it to the person on the left, saying, "With God's help, you can beat the pressure!" Have kids keep the square prayers as reminders that they can beat negative pressures.

Wrap-Up Option 2

Unison Prayers *(up to 5 minutes)*

Say: Sometimes it isn't easy to make good decisions when friends disagree with you. ➤God can help us keep our true friends while still making

The Point ➤

good decisions. Let's write prayers about this.

Have each student think of a one- or two-sentence prayer and write it on a piece of paper.

Say: With all the different voices around us telling us what to do, it's often difficult to make our voices heard. But God hears each of us—no matter what the voices around us say.

Form a circle, and have students read their prayers aloud at the same time to demonstrate their individuality, followed by saying "Amen" in unison.

Extra-Time Tips

Use these extra ideas to add some creative fun to your studies. They are low-prep or no-prep ideas that work in no time!

Peer Pressure Challenge—Form two groups. Have one group act out situations in which the crowd is pressuring one person. Then have the other groups come up with positive ideas for how the person can resist the pressure. Have groups switch roles after each situation.

Pressured Partners Prayers—Have preteens form pairs. Have members share ways they feel pressure from friends or the crowd. Then have partners pray for each other, asking for God's strength to resist the pressure.

Positive Pressure

You can avoid peer pressure without turning your friends off by using one of the following responses. In your groups practice these responses. Have group members verbally pressure another group member to (pick one)

- go to an R-rated movie with them;
- give them the answers to a math test; or
- drink a beer at a party.

Have the person resisting pressure use one or more of the following responses to say no to the rest of the group. Take turns so each group member plays the pressured teenager.

1. Say no. Stick with your response.
2. Leave. Walk away quietly.
3. Ignore the suggestion. Either pretend you didn't hear your friend, or start talking about something else.
4. Make an excuse. Think of something else you could be doing.
5. Change the subject. Pick a topic that interests your friend.
6. Make a joke. Humor lets you say no to the pressure without threatening your friend.
7. Suggest a better idea. This will give you a way out.
8. Return the challenge. If your friend says, "If you were really my friend, you'd do it," you can say, "If you were really my friend, you wouldn't ask me to do it."

To encourage the ongoing application of the truths learned in these Bible studies, try this idea:

Pressure Partners

Have preteens pick partners they know and trust. Tell them they will be pressure partners for the next month. Explain their responsibilities:

- Write or e-mail notes of encouragement at least once a week.
- Pray for your partner at least three times a week.
- Get together with your partner to discuss how he or she has handled peer pressure.
- Attend a "Pressure Busters" meeting at the conclusion of the month.

Organize a meeting, and focus on celebrating the preteens' efforts to help their partners overcome peer pressure. Encourage preteens' ongoing commitment to their friends for positive peer-pressure support.